DALKEITH Since the War

by
Craig Statham

Bert Carruthers stands third from the left in this photograph showing the staff of Jack's Bakery. The firm existed from early in the twentieth century and was extremely popular amongst the locals. The bakehouse, shown here, was in Eskdaill Street. By 1953 it had branched out and was producing 'Dalkeith Edinburgh Rock', the popularity of which saw the shop fall behind with orders. Perhaps the rock buyers of Dalkeith concurred with the claim of the shop owner, Mr Savage, that 'rock is one of the most wholesome foods going. It is practically 100 per cent sugar'. How attitudes change!

Text © Craig Statham, 2005.
First published in the United Kingdom, 2005,
by Stenlake Publishing Ltd.,
Telephone: 01290 551122
Printed by Cordfall Ltd., Glasgow, G21 2QA

ISBN 1 84033 348 0

The publishers regret that they cannot supply copies of any pictures featured in this book.

FURTHER READING

Dalkeith Advertiser
Alex C. Lawrie, *Dalkeith Through the Ages*, 1980
Dalkeith History Society, *Old Dalkeith*, Vols I–III
David R. Smith, *The Dalkeith Tolbooth and Market Cross*, Midlothian Council Library Service, 1998
David R. Smith, *The Market Town of Dalkeith and the Corn Exchange*, Dalkeith History Society
May G. Williamson, *The Origins of Street Names in Dalkeith*, Midlothian Council Library Service, 1996
W.J. Worling, *Early Railways of the Lothians*, Midlothian District Libraries, 1992

All these books can be found at the Midlothian Council Library Service Local Studies Department at Clerk Street, Loanhead. None are available from Stenlake Publishing.

ACKNOWLEDGMENTS

I must thank all those who loaned photographs for inclusion in the book, for without them it could not have been published. There are organisations and individuals whom I must name personally, as their help went beyond what I could realistically have hoped for. Alan Reid and the staff at Midlothian Council Library Service Local Studies Department were, as always, particularly helpful and allowed publication of many photographs. Dalkeith Museum also donated a number of images and provided many of the stories that reside within these pages. David R. Smith, whose knowledge of Dalkeith is second to none, loaned photographs, was always available to answer any queries, and provided a (very) thorough proofing of the text.

The publishers wish to thank the following for permission to reproduce photographs in this book: British Red Cross, Dalkeith Branch for page 21; James Currie for page 22; Dalkeith Horticultural Society for page 37; Dalkeith Lawn Tennis Club for page 47; Dalkeith Museum for pages 2–4 (upper), 5 and 19; Express Newspapers for page 11; Brent Greene for page 48; Mr & Mrs David Hamilton for page 43; Maggie Ingram for page 36; Johnston Newspapers for page 33; K. & I. Ltd for page 8; Lodge Dalkeith Kilwinning No. 10 for page 39; Tom Martin for page 4 (lower); Iain McCarter for page 12; Midlothian Council, Local Studies Library for the front cover, the inside front cover, page 1, 7, 9, 10, 13 (both), 14–18 (both), 20 (both), 23–29 (both), 30–32, 34, 35, 38, 40, 42 (both), 45 and the back cover; David R. Smith for pages 6, 44 (both) and 46; and Craig Statham for the inside back cover.

Tom Mason, Jim Foran and Tommy Nicol, pictured here, worked on Dalkeith's rubbish collection freighter, which had first been introduced in the 1940s. It was designed much like a tram car, being steered by handles rather than a wheel. Before the town's first motorised collection, rubbish was removed by tilting buckets into an uncovered horse-drawn cart.

Opposite: Gala Days were created to give the children of the town an enjoyable day out. This photograph from 1946 shows a number of children in fancy dress. Despite scenes such as this, Dalkeith's Gala Day never gained the popularity of those in smaller close-knit communities such as Loanhead and Newtongrange. The last king and queen were crowned in 1958.

INTRODUCTION

At a point just a few miles before the North and South Esk rivers meet, a variety of communities have existed for thousands of years. The modernisations of King David I saw these expanded in the twelfth century and Dalkeith emerged. The first recorded landowners in the town were the Grahams. It was they who built the town's castle which would, two centuries later, pass to the Douglasses, and finally to the present owners, the Scotts of Buccleuch. Dalkeith Castle provided lodgings for many a monarch, the first recorded instance being the night spent there by James V. His son, James VI, was a later visitor and Charles I stayed in 1633. Although not a monarch, mention must be made of the fact that in 1745 Bonnie Prince Charlie, the Young Pretender, dined at what was by then, after rebuilding, called Dalkeith Palace, following his victory at the Battle of Prestonpans. King George IV stayed in 1822, Queen Victoria in 1842 and, finally, Edward VII in 1903.

The Civil War period of the seventeenth century saw Cromwell using the town for five years as his Scottish headquarters and to barrack his army. In the twentieth century the castle has housed a Signalling School during the First World War, and the Durham Light Infantry and Polish soldiers during the Second World War.

Dalkeith emerged from the Second World War as a town undergoing enormous changes. The Woodburn housing estate was being built to the south and plans were afoot to extend it further. Taking advantage of various parliamentary Acts it was decided that the worst of the town's slums would be torn down, the town modernised and new housing built. The natural choice of replacement would have been dozens of new houses, but, with the housing problem alleviated by the building of Woodburn, it was decided to create a pedestrian-friendly town centre. Although many of the buildings nowadays elicit little but disparaging comments, attitudes at the time were mainly positive.

And the building work was to continue. Woodburn steadily grew in size. Dalkeith High and St David's High were erected, to be moved again recently to the community campus built on the town's hinterland behind Thornybank Industrial Estate. Meanwhile, the town's population continued to grow.

The work and social lives of the common people of Dalkeith mirrors that of many towns throughout Scotland. They worked in small cottage industries, making goods for sale at the local market, until the onset of the Industrial Revolution meant that the town's proximity to the Esk rivers saw the development of industries desperate for local workers. As the town and its population expanded, some began to band together to protect themselves; first into exclusive trade incorporations such as the Hammermen and the Shoemakers and then, as the Industrial Revolution and the Reform Acts began to have a positive effect on the lives of the townspeople, into inclusive friendly societies such as the Free Gardeners, Oddfellows, and Foresters. Such societies, founded on the principle of creating a financial safety net (with a strong social aspect) for the pious and temperate working men (and later women) of the town, began to decline with the introduction of the Liberal reforms of the twentieth century. But before the age of television, people still needed some form of social interaction and began to form a greater number of leisure societies. Most are now little more than a footnote in the *Dalkeith Advertiser*, but others, such as the Woodburn (Dalkeith) Ladies are recorded for posterity in photographs. Indeed some, such as the Dalkeith British Legion (Women's Section), still exist.

In recent years vast changes have again begun to overtake the town. Many of its local shops have closed, replaced by national superstores such as Tesco on the outskirts of the town, whilst charity shops occupy a good number of the High Street buildings. Two of the three large industries on the Thornybank Industrial Estate – Ferranti and Laidlaw & Fairgrieve – have closed, leaving only Letts Diaries. Four of the town's schools – Dalkeith High, Dalkeith St David's, Lugton and Westfield – have been closed and the pupils moved to the new community campus at Thornyhall. The long-standing community nursery, where so many of the town's

children (including the author) spent the mornings of their formative years, was recently closed by Midlothian Council, to be re-opened privately by the parents of the attending children. Proposals are also in place to redesign Eskdaill Court. Dalkeith House now houses an annexe of the University of Wisconsin – playing home to around 200 American students every year

Dalkeith's first pipe band was formed before the First World War. The town's second pipe band was borne out of the Army Cadet force, run by Captain Eckford, during the Second World War. It eventually split into cadet and civilian bands, although both were made up of the same members. Wullie Hall was brought in as pipe major and instructor. The first lessons were held at Dalkeith High School (when it was housed within the King's Park building) and pipes were soon purchased. Drums proved a greater problem, but three First World War kettle drums were scrounged by Captain Eckford, although the band was a little embarrassed by these at their first public appearance, playing 'Highland Laddie' along the High Street. The kettle drums were later replaced by rope drums. After only a year of practicing, the band won its first competition in Edinburgh, the

since 1986. And this modest, small town, frequented by kings and queens, but housing mainly miners and industrial workers, has become a thriving dormitory town to Edinburgh. The surging house prices in the capital have had a trickle-down effect, leaving Dalkeith with some of the highest average house prices in Scotland.

prize being a mace. But the band still had no uniforms and Peter Heriot was brought in to raise money to solve this problem. Band members trawled the town's pubs on Saturday nights (from the Unicorn to the Justinlees) with their collecting tins, and ran dances and sweeps. Eventually they raised the £100 necessary to buy the uniforms and the members were measured for McBeth tartan outfits at Jardines in Edinburgh. These two photographs show the band before they raised the money to purchase their uniforms. The sentry box in the photograph of them marching through the Duke's Gates at Dalkeith House, led by Bill Cockburn, probably dates this image to the around the time of the Second World War. The other photograph shows them making their way down Newmills Road towards Woodburn, the evening before the 1947 Gala Day.

Lagging years behind many Midlothian towns, Dalkeith did not have a Children's Day (later called the Gala Day) until 1912. The early years saw only a queen being crowned, but a king was added in 1935. This photograph shows the 1947 court with Elizabeth Hill taking her place as queen. King Richard Nelson is missing however. It is believed he was overcome with nerves and failed to take part in the ceremony, leading to many a wit remarking that he had abdicated.

In the early 1960s the town council argued that an old people's welfare hall should be opened in Dalkeith. Traders and local people decided that a barbecue was one way of raising part of the required £5,500. The first event, in 1962, was opened by Charlie Sim and Moira Briody of Scottish Television's One O'Clock Gang and raised between £800 and £900. The day ended, as they have ever since, with a bonfire and fireworks display. Councillor William Stewart called it 'the biggest thing to hit Dalkeith in all its history'. The hall was opened, and still exists, as part of the building housing the medical centre in St Andrews Street. This photograph shows the opening parade of the 1993 event passing through the east end of the High Street. Sitting in the car is Ronnie Browne of the Corries, who opened the event that year. Other celebrities who have had the honour include children's entertainer Glen Michael, and Jim Aitken, captain of the 1984 Grand Slam-winning Scottish rugby team.

The Dalkeith branch of the Royal British Legion was founded after the end of the First World War. A Women's Section was formed in 1932 by six members. At the time of its 'coming-of-age' in 1953 it had forty members. The 21st birthday party was held in the Unicorn Inn. A cake was donated by Mrs E.E.R. Noble, the Honorary President, who also cut it with the help of Mrs P. Finlay, the President. To round the evening off members sang songs and music was provided by Drummond's Band. It is likely that this photograph was taken during the 1940s. Both the flags displayed in the background still exist and are currently displayed at the society's premises in Buccleuch Street.

In 1898 James Kirkness and Sandy Innes set up a works in Leith to manufacture and maintain specialist handcrafted motor-bodies, trailers and handcarts. Later expansions of Kirkness and Innes (known generally as K. & I. Ltd) saw further works opened at Eskbank and Viewforth. This photograph shows the staff of the Eskbank works in 1948, soon after its opening. In the early years the hangar on the right was part of the premises, but was later replaced. The chimney at the top of the photograph belongs to Henry Widnell and Stewart's carpet factory. Whilst building specialist vehicles has remained a core feature of the company's business, in recent years they have diversified to incorporate a changing market. This has seen the creation of a car repair centre and the design of vehicle signs. The fact the company still exists today is due in part to their innovative approach to business – they built the first National Blood Transfusion van, the first mine rescue vehicle (for NCB Coatbridge) and numerous mobile banks for the Highlands and Islands of Scotland and the Middle East.

The buildings in the High Street on the right of this photograph were to succumb to the scourges of re-development in the 1960s. All the other buildings remain, albeit under different ownership. Forrest's Bar (now Mackay's) was a highly popular public house. It had existed since 1870, but gained its popular name after James Forrest took over in 1915, although he later changed its name to the Victoria Bar. After his death in 1944 his daughters, Betty and Agnes, took over its running.

In the early part of the twentieth century royal visits and coronations were met with an outpouring of joy and celebration. Dalkeith would be bedecked with an array of Union flags and bunting. By the time of Queen Elizabeth's coronation in 1953, however, the monarchy had become a source of much contention. The problem began when local businessmen threatened to withdraw their support for the coronation celebrations because the crowning of the Gala Day king and queen was planned for the same day. Thirty-seven shopkeepers signed a petition arguing that this was 'an insult to the Queen'. Councillor David R. Smith fanned the flames further by announcing he was a republican and he repudiated 'the whole idea of having any hereditary royal family'. Arguments raged via the *Dalkeith Advertiser* for several weeks, but in April the businessmen finally relented and agreed to support the event 'so the children would not suffer'. Robert Hutchison, a local draper, offered to pay for 2,000 coronation flags for the town's children but the offer was promptly turned down by the Coronation Committee. The businessmen accused the council of being unpatriotic, the council responding that there were 3,000 children in the town – 1,000 more children than flags. The town's children did eventually receive a number of free gifts. Robert Hutchison handed out 1,500 flags and pencils inside two hours, with a further 500 of each going to local organisations. Joseph Smith, a local fish restaurant proprietor, provided 3*d.* and 4*d.* bags of chips for 1,248 children. Lastly, Mr Pryde, of Pryde and Scott radio and television dealers, handed out red, white and blue paper hats. This photograph was taken in King's Park on the day of the coronation, and Dalkeith Burgh Band can be seen on the right. The crowd was smaller than expected – this being blamed on television coverage and the poor weather, which caused many events to be cancelled at King's Park. Although the crowd swelled for the actual crowning of the Gala Day king and queen, it quickly reduced after the event and band performances at King's Park and at Woodburn Amphitheatre were given before small numbers.

Until relatively recently, royal visits by the monarch to Dalkeith were a frequent occurrence. This photograph was taken during the last one in July 1961, when the Queen and Prince Philip visited the town. The visitors' book they are signing still exists. During their scheduled 16-minute stay they met with an array of local dignitaries. It was standing room only at Crystal Mount for those viewing the events, so much so that many watched from the roof of the adjacent S.M.T. bus garage. After signing the visitors' book, the royal party left for Bonnyrigg. Shortly after their departure, Provost Moffat, who had welcomed the visitors, collapsed and was rushed to the Edinburgh Royal Infirmary. He died three months later.

John McCarter was born at Newmills, Dalkeith, in 1894. Whilst working at his father's slater's business the First World War broke out and he signed up immediately with the eighth Royal Scots. He returned from the war unscathed and continued to work in the building trade. At this time he was taking violin lessons, but his teacher noted that he should perhaps make violins rather than play them! However, Mr McCarter took the teacher's word and set out to make his own violins, creating the instruments in his workshop, shown here, at the rear of his house in Glebe Street. Over the years he made approximately twenty violins and most of them remain with his family, although he gave one to Ian Powrie,

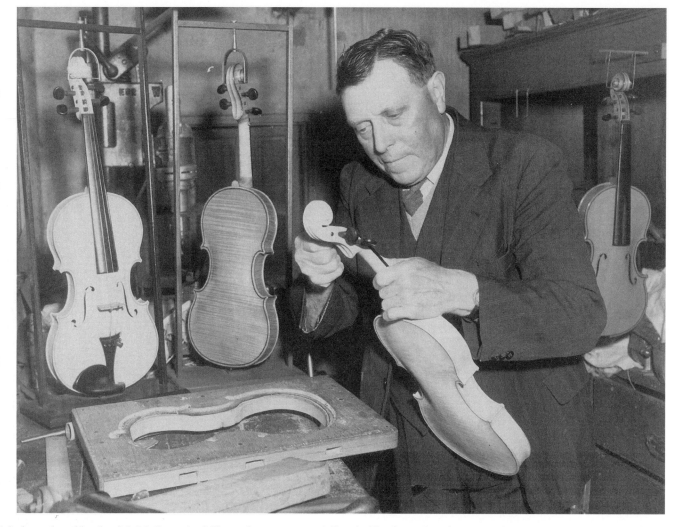

the well-known Scottish dance band leader. Mr McCarter's skill, at what was essentially a hobby, brought admiration from many quarters. Vic Oliver, the entertainer, remarked how impressed he was by their high standard and Sir Robert Lorimer, architect of the Scottish National War Memorial, also praised his workmanship. Mr McCarter continued to work in the building trade in Dalkeith well into his seventies and died, aged 92, in 1987.

Since its grand opening in 1854 the Corn Exchange has hosted an eclectic range of meetings, social events and industries. Around 3,000 people crammed in to listen to William Gladstone speaking there during his 'Midlothian Campaign' of 1878. Winston Churchill also spoke there in 1904, albeit to a smaller crowd of around 1,000. In 1946 it was used for regular dances and called the Empress Ballroom. Its opening attracted a crowd of 700, with music being provided by Cam Robbie and his Melody Makers. The ballroom's lease expired in 1961. These photographs are believed to show it being dismantled, in preparation for its conversation to a training annexe to Ferranti's newly built factory at Thornybank.

This photograph shows Hepburn Drive in the Woodburn Estate, named after John Hepburn, Provost of the council from 1938 to 1941. Built in 1954, it has changed little over the years, although there are now more parked cars and speed humps. When the Labour Party took control of the town council for the first time in 1935 the issue of Dalkeith's slum housing was fully appreciated. The policies of Woodburn Estate offered an attractive solution. For many years after it was built in 1793, Woodburn House stood resplendent in its vast grounds to the south of Dalkeith. By 1934 it was derelict and the estate was purchased for the princely sum of £5,500. The first streets to be built were Woodburn Drive, Woodburn Road and Spalding Crescent. The demolition of Woodburn House created further space. The entrance pillars were moved and can now be seen opposite the post office in Woodburn Road. From 1945 the housing development began to spread further south. The Cowden estate followed soon after. This tackling of the housing problem led E. G. Willis, the Secretary of State for Scotland, to note in 1965 that Dalkeith was 'tackling the problem of housing with more vigour and sense of purpose than almost any other burgh in Scotland'. But the building work did not stop. In 1974 a number of additional streets were erected, from Whitehill Drive southwards. Despite being given such historically evocative names as Robert Burns' Mews, Clarinda Gardens (named after an Edinburgh lady who corresponded with Burns), Pankhurst Loan (named after the three suffragettes) and Jean Armour Drive (named after Burns's wife) it soon gained the nickname Colditz due to its being so hard to find individual houses and then to find a way out!

The building of the Woodburn estate led to the creation of the Woodburn (Dalkeith) Ladies' Social Club, pictured here during a fancy dress evening. The club was formed by the town's district nurses at the clinic in Woodburn Road and continued to function after the nurses left the district. At the time of their fifteenth anniversary the club had over forty members. They received talks from a variety of organisations, donated monies to many charities, had numerous social evenings, and took children and grandchildren on annual trips to local beaches. One of these day-trippers remembers taking what is possibly the last train out of Dalkeith Station, to Burntisland, in the early 1960s. So decrepit was the line that a guard had to walk in front of the train until it reached Eskbank.

Dalkeith's first Methodist Church was established in 1786 by Zachariah Yewdall. Three years later he organised the building of the congregation's first chapel, on land purchased for the price of £26 10/- in the area now known as South Street. It would become known as the Wesley Hall. In 1960 the Dalkeith building was purchased by the council for £1,500 and soon demolished. The town's second Methodist church, the Westfield Chapel, built in 1886 and a far grander building, was demolished five years later, although it had not been used since the 1920s.

This photograph was taken from what is now Eskdaill Court and shows the entrance into Back Street. On the right stands the Old Mealmarket Inn, one of the town's oldest known drinking establishments.

OLD MEAL MARKET
— INN —
Wᴹ YOUNGER'S
CELEBRATED ALES
IN BOTTLE & ON DRAUGHT

A.B. STEVENS
WINES AND SPIRITS

St Andrews Street was known as Back Street until 1958, when it was largely rebuilt. The author's grandmother was born at No. 89 in 1909.

There is evidence of a brewery existing in Dalkeith as early as 1789. In 1887 McLennan and Urquhart acquired the site at the west end of Back Street and one of the most enduring and famous of Dalkeith's industrial companies was born. It soon flourished, due in great part to its well-regarded beers, facilitating the purchase of additional properties throughout Scotland. By the 1950s it employed fifty people. It was awarded a Royal Warrant in 1951 for supplying bottled ales to Balmoral, although the Royal coat-of-arms that adorned the building was bought second-hand. This, and the installation of an automatic bottling and pasteurising plant soon after, seemed to mark the turning point in the company's fortunes. In 1955 it was bought over by Aitchison's of Edinburgh, who continued to use the Dalkeith premises. Work was, however, gradually wound down and ceased altogether in 1961. When no longer in use, the buildings, shown in these photographs, were damaged by a fire and finally demolished in the late 1960s.

Dalkeith High School, under various guises, has existed since 1582 or earlier. It was based in a number of buildings until 1912, when it moved to King's Park School where it remained for almost half a century. In the 1950s increasing pupil numbers forced the purpose-building of a school in Newmills Road, on a strip of land behind the new Burgh School, between Allan Terrace, in the background, and the old fever hospital and allotments (the latter now replaced by another house) in the foreground. The main contractors were the local firm of John Monteith and this photograph shows the building in the early stages of construction. After completion, a sculptured prima ballerina was affixed to the

swimming pool wall and served as a metaphor for everything it was hoped students would aspire to. John S. MacLay, the Secretary of State for Scotland, officially opened the new school in 1960. It was one of four local schools – alongside St David's, Lugton, and Westfield – closed in 2004. The students are now based at Scotland's first joint campus, sited at Thornyhall. The old Dalkeith High building is listed, which may save it from demolition.

In the post-war years there were attempts in the highest political circles throughout Europe to promote fraternity between nations, and the twinning of towns was seen as a way to promote this. In 1958 a Dalkeith councillor, James Quinn, wrote to the United Towns Organisation in Paris requesting that a suitable twinning partner be found. At this time the French town of Jarnac was also seeking a twinning partner and a long association was begun. The following year members of the twinning committee visited the town of Jarnac in the Charente region to formalise the arrangement. A reciprocal visit followed in 1960 and week-long celebrations were organised. They were called 'Jarnac Week'. The French party were greeted at the Corn Exchange by the Burgh Band, and then taken to the Municipal Buildings at the northern end of Buccleuch Street. Provost Thomas Lean and Jarnac's Deputy Mayor, Maurice Voiron, stood on the balcony and the band played the Marseillaise and God Save the Queen to a crowd of hundreds. The officials then moved to Melville Castle Hotel for an official dinner. Jarnac officials were presented with a gavel and tray made from oak grown on the Buccleuch Estate. The following week Provost Thomas Lean spoke of the success of the event, describing the visitors as 'people akin to ourselves'. Another Scottish visit to France later that year saw the presentation of a charter by the French Mayor, M. Fougerat, which noted that it was hoped the twinning would create 'a lasting friendship and aspire to the development of our mutual interests to the greater happiness of all'. In 1965, at the height of the Cold War, Maurice Voiron, Deputy Mayor of Jarnac, noted 'governments can argue over atomic warfare. But we the people can chat together about the ordinary things that are important to us. This can be done through twinning committees'. This photograph shows the twinning ceremony in King's Park. Visitors were accorded great formality, as can be seen by their being led through the town by a pipe band.

Various means have been used to care for the sick and poorly of Dalkeith. A Board of Health was established in 1831, a fever hospital opened in 1882, a District Nursing Association was founded in 1895, and a Child Welfare Clinic opened in 1920. This photograph shows the Dalkeith branch of the British Red Cross, taken in October 1960 on its fiftieth anniversary in the Buccleuch Street church hall. Lady Rosebery headed a list of distinguished guests. The detachment and cadets, who numbered fifty, are awaiting inspection.

The railway line passing Dalkeith was opened in 1831. Seven years later a branch line was built into the town – the station being roughly where the First Bus garage is today. Its early role as a goods railway was soon supplemented by passenger services, but from 1942 until the 1960s, when it was finally closed, the line carried mainly freight. Occasionally, however, passenger trains were granted permission to use the line. This photograph from August 1962 shows a train filled with members of the Stephenson Locomotive Society on a railtour.

From early times Dalkeith was a maze of closes, most linking the High Street and Back Street in the east end of the town. They were a breeding ground for poverty and disease, and many, including Candlemaker Close, and Amos's Close were eventually torn down. Some, however, do remain. This photograph looks towards Back Street through Robertson's Close.

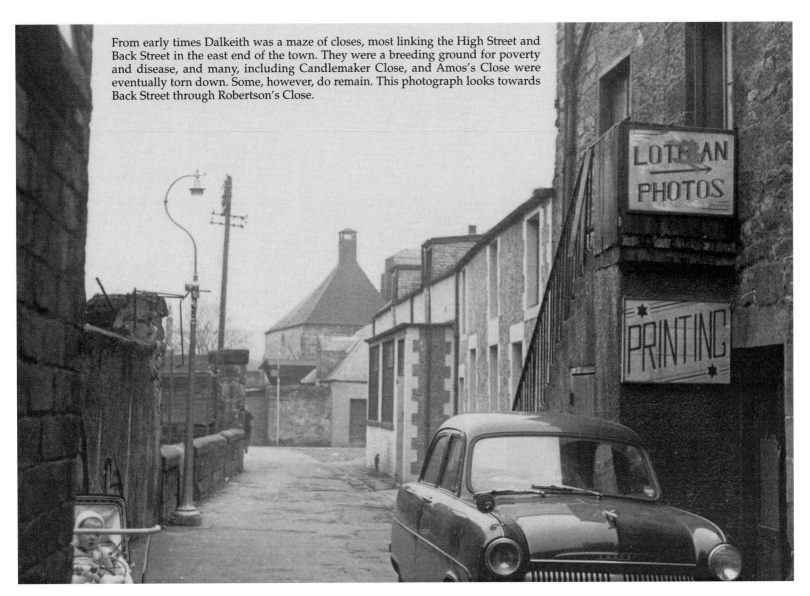

By 1959 the shops in Dalkeith town centre were facing a rapid decline in trade so a plan was conceived to re-develop the area. The primary aim of the plan was to remove the buildings within the 'square' formed by the High Street, Buccleuch Street, Lothian Street and South Street (virtually every building was demolished) and to create aesthetically pleasing open spaces with housing incorporated. This was done through the creation of three 'squares' – Jarnac Court, Eskdaill Court, and Komarom Court. These two photographs show the row of shops on the High Street which faced onto the buildings now housing W. H. Smith and the Royal Bank of Scotland. They were demolished in the 1960s. From left they are Baird the clothier, Renton the hairdresser, Jim Smith the newsagent, Central Cycles, Shillinglaw's wallpaper shop, and Laing's hardwares.

The lady and her children are crossing South Street from the direction of the Old Mealmarket Inn towards what is now Eskdaill Court. The shop on the left, advertising the Bee Gees at Rosewell Miners' Welfare, was best known as Grant's, the second-hand furnisher. Hoy's paint shop is in the centre, whilst the one on the right was best known as Tom Hall's butcher shop. At the time of the photograph the buildings were being readied for demolition as part of Phase III of the town re-development programme of the 1960s.

Walking from Tom Hall's towards the High Street would take one past Ellis's clothing shop and the well-known Bell Brothers bakery.

The line of White Hart Street, photographed here and on the following two pages, was retained when many of the buildings within it were demolished and replaced by a modern shopping centre. One of the best known buildings in the street before re-development was the Assembly Hall, which was associated with the White Hart Inn. In 1880 it was taken over by local Conservatives and became the Unionist Club. At the far end of the street can be seen the Playhouse Cinema in Buccleuch Street. After its closure it was taken over for use as the Corner Pocket Snooker Club and has witnessed the skills of such stars as the 'housewives' favourite' Tony Knowles. The last of these photographs, showing David Scott's newsagents', is taken looking from Buccleuch Street, the car park sitting roughly where Dalkeith Library is today.

In 1965 Phase I of the re-development was completed. One observer of post-Second World War architecture noted that 'the dead hand of drab uniformity has throttled the life out of what was the best in the culture and heritage of our older towns. Speculation and commercialism have done what Hitler's bombs failed to do . . . devastated the most characteristic and aesthetic features of our architectural tradition'. Thankfully, Dalkeith avoided such failings. Gone, announced Provost David Smith, was a 'dismal, horrible conglomeration of ramshackle property . . . evil slums which mentally crippled our people . . . dark, dingy and treacherous closes [replaced by] a masterpiece of local achievement'. Their replacement – Jarnac Court – was opened by Maurice Voiron, Deputy Mayor of Jarnac. E. G. Willis, the Secretary of State for Scotland, opened the council chambers. He noted that they would be 'looked upon by the people of Dalkeith with a friendly regard'. In the thirty years since the Labour Party had taken over Dalkeith Town Council over 800 residences had been demolished. Gone forever were the slums, but we should perhaps mourn the disappearance of evocative and colourful street names such as Hammermen's Land, The Wicket, and Candlework Close. The creation of Jarnac Court cost £150,000.

At the grand opening of Jarnac Court Dalkeith Burgh Band played before an array of invited guests and local onlookers. In the evening a meal was held at the Melville Castle Hotel. Several notables made speeches, including Maurice Voiron, Deputy Mayor of Jarnac. Note the French flag on the table.

Many felt that the 1960s re-development of Dalkeith town centre should have included a large degree of restoration. Councillor David R. Smith noted that for a variety of reasons this was not feasible, but he did argue that the building on the right of this photograph should be retained. However, its crumbling state dictated its demolition, along with the other buildings seen here. In 1969 the Newbattle Press Bureau (which took this photograph) and the Government Surplus Store (both built in 1750) and Deans's Newsagent (erected at a later date) were removed. Their destruction, however, opened up to public view a number of cottages in Brunton's Close. It was decided that, despite their poor condition, restoration was a valid option. The results can still be viewed today, providing a pleasant outlook on the northern side of east High Street.

In the early nineteenth century farmers from the Dalkeith area formed an agricultural society and it is likely that their annual show was organised soon after. In recent years venues for the event have included Thornybank, Elmfield Park, King's Park and, most recently, Westgate Park in Lugton. Despite poor weather the 1965 event, shown here, was still a success. The society's president, the Duke of Buccleuch, arrived early and was shown around the numerous attractions. Judging of the animals continued throughout the day, with the champions being shown in this photograph. A range of other events kept the less agriculturally minded occupied. For the children there was a fancy dress parade and a model railway, whilst the Dalkeith men took on, and lost to, East Lothian in a tug-of-war competition.

In 1779 the first brush was sold by James Dawson and Co. and it would be almost 200 years before the last was sold. A vast array of brush types was produced for a range of different buyers. The post-war years brought a shortage of the preferred tropical hardwoods used to make the brush handles, and they were replaced by Russian and memel oaks. The best bristles were derived from Chinese and Indian pigs – supposedly the wilder the pig, the better the bristle. This photograph, showing employee Bob Robertson, is believed to have been taken in 1967. The factory in Dalkeith's High Street closed in 1972 and the company spent a short spell in Croft Street before closing its doors for the last time.

Many Scottish towns and burghs have a tolbooth, a building that housed the jail and where much of the local administration was carried out. Dalkeith's first tolbooth was contained within the sacristy of the parish church. It was replaced by this building in the early eighteenth century. The stone tablet on the front of the building, dated 1648, was probably taken from Dalkeith Castle. William Thomson, a labourer, had the unenviable 'honour' of being the last person to be executed in Dalkeith (for mugging a farmer), and the stone circle of setts where this event took place are still visible in front of the building. The tolbooth was not suddenly replaced, but rather began to be increasingly used for other purposes in the nineteenth century. By 1870 it had become known as the Scientific Hall and became a meeting place for a range of societies including the Co-operative Society, the Horticultural Society, the tennis club, and an array of political groups.

A cell to hold prisoners can still be found in Dalkeith's old tolbooth. In 1841 a new prison was opened in West Wynd, but in 1878 the police force moved once more, to the old Militia Barracks (roughly where Lauder Lodge stands today). It was here that Tom 'Reidie' Seath, pictured here with the Edinburgh City Police Pipe Band playing outside the Advocates' Library in Parliament Square, Edinburgh, would have served as a sergeant. He was an accomplished piper and a popular and respected figure in the town. The current police station, next to Esk Valley College, was opened in 1980.

The earliest known mention of the Dalkeith Horticultural Society was in the *Scottish Gardener* magazine in 1861. The article detailed the society's annual summer competition at the Corn Exchange. The society must have closed down soon after as the *Dalkeith Advertiser* noted in 1871 that local gardeners were meeting to re-form it. During the 1950s and 1960s the Dalkeith Flower Show was held in a marquee in King's Park. After this, several venues were used including Buccleuch Street church hall, Dobbies' Garden Centre, Esk Valley College, and St David's High School. The society's annual show in September 1969 attracted over 3,000 people. Rikki Fulton, the Scottish comedian is standing beside Miss Scotland, presenting a prize to an exhibitor. The show was recorded by BBC Scotland and broadcast as part of *The Scottish Garden* series. This was not Fulton's first visit to the town. In 1963 he had opened the Barbecue with fellow comedian Jack Milton.

This photograph shows the premises of John Hope and Son Ltd, engineers and brassfounders, in the town's North Wynd. The company was created in 1864 by John Hope and remained in his family until just before the First World War. In 1947 the company constructed a miniature paper-making machine. Designed by Mr Francis W. Gray of Eskbank, it was 60 feet long and 18 inches wide. This link with the paper industry was to provide the foundation for the majority of the company's business and helped open up the world market, with machines being exported to France, Belgium, Greece, India and Romania. The company was closed in the late 1960s or early 1970s. The building, however, still exists, housing Edinburgh Sportscars, although the chimney stack is somewhat smaller and no longer functions. The houses beyond, in Relief Place, were demolished after being described as 'uninhabitable' in the 1967/68 valuation rolls. Their site was taken by Dalkeith Baptist Church.

It is believed that freemasonry in Dalkeith dates to the seventeenth century, the minute books of the Melrose Lodge noting that James Mein had been entered at Dalkeith in 1681. Officially, Lodge Dalkeith Kilwinning No. 10 (originally No. 9) is recognised as having been founded in 1724 and it celebrated its 250th anniversary in 1974. During the anniversary day members of the lodge and invited guests attended a service at St Nicholas Church and marched along the town's High Street. During the events they wore their full regalia and carried the lodge banner. Dating from after 1816, the banner bears three Latin inscriptions *Memento Mori* (Be Mindful of Death), *Sapientia Constans* (Ever Wise) and *Cenceo Nulli* (I Yield to No-one). Some days later an evening meal was enjoyed at the Community Centre in Woodburn Road.

The chapel of St Mary's was commissioned by the fifth Duke of Buccleuch and built between 1843 and 1845 with stone from Cowden quarry. Its English college chapel style has led the sacristan to call it 'an elderly lady in period clothing'. The sounds which emanate from it are borne from a Hamilton organ which is run hydraulically by wind and water. It is nowadays looked after by the Liverpool firm Rushforth and Dreaper. Post-war events cannot perhaps equal the excitement of a night in 1913 when suffragettes attempted to blow up the building, but deserve to be mentioned in the town's history. In 1980 the incumbent minister, Mr Stuart Chedburn, retired, and the church was linked with St Leonard's of Lasswade. In October 1981 Richard, Earl of Dalkeith, married Lady Elizabeth Kerr. Around 1,000 guests travelled from around the world, although only 200 could fit into the chapel for the ceremony, which was conducted by Bishop Alistair Haggart, Primus of the Episcopalian Church in Scotland. The most notable guests were Princess Anne and Captain Mark Phillips. In recent years one of the gargoyles fell from the wall. It portrays a man with toothache!

Dalkeith became a Burgh of Barony in 1401. In later years it was made a Burgh of Regality. In 1878 it was granted the status of police burgh, allowing it to elect a representative council, raise taxes and carry out statutory services. A hundred years later Dalkeith celebrated the award of its burgh status by holding a civic event called 'Dalkeith 100 Week'. Coordinated by Dalkeith and District Round Table, events such as Superstars, rugby, football, a pram race, a fancy dress competition, and music by a range of pipe and silver bands made the week a memorable one. This photograph shows John Watson, the town crier, during the festival as he walked through Jarnac Court ringing a bell and reading a proclamation. Around him are members of the Round Table, handing out leaflets advertising the event. The week was rounded off with the annual Barbecue, opened by Radio Forth DJ Jay Crawford.

A major event within the 100 Week festivities was the holding of an exhibition in the arts centre. Opened by 92-year-old Jimmy Gillan, it included a number of displays celebrating Dalkeith's history. Amongst other facts, visitors learned – although it is probably an exaggeration – that early traffic could travel no faster than four miles per hour through the town, following a man walking with a red flag. The display shown in this photograph was put together by 'E' division of the Lothian and Borders police. The 'policeman' stands with a birch. Those found guilty of a crime in old Dalkeith would have been tied to the birching stand, also shown, and punished.

In August 1926 5,000 striking miners converged on King's Park to listen to the radical union leader A.J. Cook speaking during the Miners' Strike, which had grown out of the General Strike. Almost sixty years later, between 1984 and 1985, the country was once again torn apart by a national strike – although this one was confined to the mining industry. As a community strongly founded on mining tradition, Dalkeith provided a solid base of support for those who spent a year without wages. In 1984 Arthur Scargill, president of the National Union of Mineworkers, came to Dalkeith to make a speech. A vast procession made its way from King's Park to Cowden Park via the Miners' Club at Woodburn. After avoiding being hit by an egg en route, Scargill took his place on a wooden stage which had been erected some days before the event. Beside him were Alex Eadie MP, George Bolton, and Ella Egan, on the right, who was the daughter of the renowned miners' leader Abe Moffat. Behind the stage stood an array of miners' banners, whilst in front a crowd of 4,000 to 5,000 listened to Scargill declaring that 'together, united, we will never be defeated'.

Midlothian District Council took a strong public stance against apartheid. They supported a national campaign that boycotted goods from South Africa or Namibia and supported the withdrawal of all investment from South African companies. In December 1985 they held an Anti-apartheid Day. Speakers included the Scottish Labour MP Judith Hart and Reverend Bethlehem Nopece, a minister from South Africa, both shown here with members of the council. The attendees watched the film *Island* which views South Africa through the eyes of inmates of Robben Island prison, where Nelson Mandela was held. Mandela was later awarded the honorary freedom of Midlothian 'in recognition of his substantial contribution to the struggle against denial of human rights'.

In the first half of the nineteenth century there was a constant demand from Edinburgh's College of Surgeons for fresh cadavers. And so emerged the resurrectionists, also known as 'grave-robbers', 'body snatchers' and 'sack-em-up men', intent on supplying this demand for a profit. Dalkeith, it seemed, had cause to remain

vigilant. In D.M. Moir's book entitled *Mansie Waugh*, Dalkeith's eponymous tailor noted that there was 'a great sough and surmise that some loons were playing false with the kirkyard, howking up the bodies from their damp graves and harling them away to the College'. To protect the newly buried, a watchtower was built in the graveyard in 1827. The 'Committee for the Protection of the New Burying Ground', which erected the structure, noted that it was necessary due to 'certain monsters who practiced the disinterring of the dead bodies'. Armed guards stood watch from the upper floor. In more recent years it was used as to store the equipment and materials of the town's gravediggers. In 1984 the structure was restored by the Manpower Services Commission with the costs met by the Common Good Fund, Dalkeith Community Council, and Dalkeith History Society. To commemorate its re-opening in the spring of 1986 Dr Owen Dudley-Edwards of the University of Edinburgh, having recently written a book about the murderers Burke and Hare, was invited to make a speech, in which he quoted Robert Louis Stevenson and Sir Walter Scott. This photograph shows David Smith and members of the History Society listening to Dr Dudley-Edwards at the door of the tower. It is currently part of the town's History Trail which also incorporates Dalkeith House, St Mary's Chapel, the Corn Exchange, and the tolbooth.

In the early twentieth century photographers would visit Dalkeith and their work would be published as picture postcards. Most would, inevitably, take one of the town from the High Woods. This image shows the area in the post-Second World War period when the public park below the woods was being used by the Burgh School, which stood at the west end of Mitchell Street.

This building on Edinburgh Road was erected in 1870 and originally housed Alexander Mitchell's merchants' store. Mitchell was to become the town's first provost and his house still stands just a few yards further down the road, now bearing a plaque in his honour. The Full Gospel Church was one of many groups to have occupied this building; at present it is occupied by Alzheimer Scotland.

Dalkeith Lawn Tennis Club is one of the town's longest-running but least well known social institutions. It is tucked away near the old water tower on Eskbank Road, now a private house and shown in the background of this photograph. A share certificate shows that the club was in existence in 1888, but the land which it presently owns was acquired from the Duke of Buccleuch in 1920 for £50, after initially being rented from him. The inaugural meeting, held on 20 June of that year, was opened by J.C. Sturrock. The pavilion, from where this photograph was taken, proved to be inadequate, with no 'sanitary arrangements' available, in 1922. A year later a kitchen, ladies' room and storeroom were added to the rear and a verandah to the front. During the Second World War the grounds were requisitioned for use by the War Department, although they were never used.

Since 1986 American students from four (later five) University of Wisconsin colleges – La Crosse, Eau Claire, Stout, River Falls and Superior – have studied at Dalkeith House. The university uses the house as an annexe to allow students to broaden both their education and horizons. Time is set aside for travel, and many make their way to Europe. A student in one of the first groups, Steve Zagzebski, remembers 'the experience I had in Dalkeith continues to be the highlight of my life'. This picture shows the group who visited in June 2004.